COPYRIGHTS

C000165920

The First Edition was granted an imprimatur in November 2006 as seen below. Revisions to this text have been limited to modifications based on the new translation of the Roman Missal. No other changes have been made to the First Edition.

Nihil obstat: Rev. Theodore R. Book, S.L.L. 3 November, 2006.
Imprimatur: †Most Rev. Wilton D. Gregory, S.L.D., Archbishop of Atlanta,
7 November, 2006
The *Nihil obstat* and *Imprimatur* are a declaration that a book or pamphlet is   considered to be free from doctrinal or moral error. It is not implied that those who have granted the *Nihil obstat* and *Imprimatur* agree with the contents, opinions,   or statements expressd.

Originally Printed in Color in February 2007

THE CATHOLIC MASS...*REVEALED!*

TABLE OF CONTENTS

THE CATHOLIC MASS...*REVEALED!*

THE CATHOLIC MASS... REVEALED!

T he Catholic Mass is the most sacred act of worship a person can participate in on earth. The night before He died, the Lord Jesus Christ sat down with His twelve chosen apostles for what He knew would be their last meal together. At that supper, Jesus did something new, something never done before and yet something that would continue from that day until the end of time. He gave us the Food of eternal life. He instituted the Holy Mass.

Knowing more about the Mass, we can be closer to Christ and to the Miracle He left us on that Holy Thursday night.

The Catholic Mass...Revealed! is designed to help you learn more about the Mass. By helping all people, both Catholics and non-Catholics, to better understand the Mass, we hope to lead you to appreciate this greatest of all gifts, its beauty and rhythm, and even why many saints in history have faced death rather than to be deprived of the opportunity to participate in the Mass.

Our prayer is that you will come to know and love the Mass for what it truly is – making present again what Jesus did at the Last Supper and an offering to the Father, Jesus' sacrifice co-joined with our own. As you grow to understand the Mass, you will come to know and love Jesus Himself – He who both invites and commands us to encounter Him in this very special way.

CHAPTER 1

PREPARING FOR MASS

When we attend a sporting event or a concert, we prepare for it. We may wear a cap with the logo of our favorite team or read up on the band. On the way, we discuss with our friends how great it will be. When we go to Mass, we are meeting

with God Himself. So, we want to prepare for Mass, for this special meeting with Jesus.

We need to prepare our minds and souls for the wonders contained in every Mass, whether in a grand Cathedral or a humble chapel.

The best preparation for Mass is prayer. We should try to arrive to Mass early. Be silent and reflective. Ask the Lord to give you His peace to assist you in removing distractions, worries, and anxieties. Think of how much you need God. Think of an intention for which to offer the Mass. Thank God for inviting you to come to Mass. Think of how you would like to offer yourself by desiring to do His will, just as Christ prayed to the Father in the Lord's Prayer: *"Thy Kingdom come, Thy will be done!"*

How would you prepare for an audience with a King or President? How well must we prepare for an audience with Jesus Himself, for He said about Himself: *"There is something greater than Solomon here."* (cf. Mt 12:42)

As we get ready, we notice that it takes time to transition ourselves from the noise of the world and our daily lives. We are often distracted at Mass. This is normal and God understands. Christ told St. Martha that she worried about many things, but only one thing was necessary: to be with Him. At Mass, we should try to be with Christ, listen to Him, and accompany Him in faith. What were Jesus' thoughts and feelings as He offered Himself for me, as He took up the Cross for me?

As WE GET READY, WE NOTICE THAT IT TAKES TIME TO TRANSITION OURSELVES FROM THE NOISE OF THE WORLD AND OUR DAILY LIVES.

"Eucharist" means *"Thanksgiving."* The Mass is a thanksgiving to God. We should prepare for Mass by thanking God for His many gifts and blessings, but above all the Gift of His Son. Let's pray to make each and every Mass a true encounter with Jesus Christ.

CHAPTER 2

INTRODUCTORY RITES

The Holy Mass makes present again the work of Redemption. Christ renews His *Last Supper, Passion, Death,* and *Resurrection* at every Mass. The Mass begins with the Introductory Rites. These Rites are a beginning, an introduction, and a preparation for the other parts of the Mass. We have been invited to the Holy Sacrifice of Christ and we are called to participate as a family. At God's family gathering, we show unity with each other and ask forgiveness for anyone we have hurt. In the Introductory Rites, we dispose ourselves to accompany Christ like the first disciples at the Last Supper when they had their feet washed by Christ before the supper began.

As Mass begins, we want to be in a state of prayer, to realize that we are in God's presence. We begin by turning to God in faith and asking for His forgiveness, so that we can be united to Him and to one another in love. Soon, the Readings will begin, followed by the Eucharistic Prayer and Communion. The Mass will end with the Concluding Rite.

The Roman Catholic Mass has two main parts: the Liturgy of the Word and the Liturgy of the Eucharist. The Word is the readings from the Holy Bible. The Eucharist is the Body and Blood of Jesus our Lord. The Church teaches that the Mass, and specifically the Eucharist, is *the source, summit, and font of the Christian life and of the whole Church.* There is nothing more important than the Mass.

The Introductory Rites come before the Liturgy of the Word at the beginning of Mass. The Mass ends after the Liturgy of the Eucharist, with the Concluding Rite. The Mass is a complete spiritual event, like

As Mass begins, we want to be in a state of prayer, to realize that we are in God's presence.

a workout complete with pre-exercise stretching and post-exercise cool down.

We are not just spectators at the Mass. We are participants. We have five activities in the Mass: we *pray*, we *listen* to God's teaching, we *offer* our gifts and ourselves to God through and with the priest, we *sacrifice*, for we join the offering of our lives to the one sacrifice of Christ offered through the hands of the priest, and finally, we *receive* Christ in Holy Communion, the Food our souls need to live in Him.[1]

The Introductory Rites include the Entrance Procession, the Greeting by the priest, the Penitential Rite for our sins, the *Kyrie* or "Lord have Mercy," the *Gloria* or "Glory to God" said on Sundays and special feast days, and the Opening Prayer, also called the "Collect."

---

[1] Cf. Daniel-Rops, Henri, This is the Mass (Hawthorn Books: New York) 1965, p. 37.

THE CATHOLIC MASS...REVEALED!

CHAPTER 3

ENTRANCE

Mass begins with a procession. The priest and the other ministers, readers, and altar servers slowly walk toward the Table of the parish family, which is also the Altar of Sacrifice. The procession can be simple or more elaborate. In some Masses in India, ceremonial elephants have even been used! Sometimes the *Entrance Antiphon* is said or sung, or the congregation sings a hymn to express our unity.

On Sundays, an image of Christ crucified and the Book of the Gospels is carried in the procession. Together with the Sacramentary and the Lectionary, these are the main books used at Mass. The Crucifix is placed on or near the altar (unless one is already there). In the Mass, we remember how Jesus said on the Cross: *"It is finished"* (cf. Jn 19:30). We remember how He consummated His Sacrifice for love of us. The crucifix also reminds us that we must carry our crosses with Jesus. He gives us the strength to live like He did, in selfless dedication to God and to others. The Gospels contain Christ's presence in his Word. In them, Jesus teaches us about His life and how to be like Him.

The beginning of Mass shows us how we must always begin all that we do in the Name of the Father, Son, and Holy Spirit, and under the sign of the Cross.

CHAPTER 4

GREETING

The Mass joins Heaven and earth. It gathers the whole Family of God. In Mass, we participate with Heaven as the Angels fall down in worship before God. Even the souls in Purgatory are aware of the blessings and graces we send them from praying for them at Mass. All of our brothers and sisters, everyone in the world, benefits from our prayers at Mass.

The priest approaches the altar and venerates it with a bow. He, together with the deacon (if there is one), also kisses the altar. This is a very ancient practice. It shows adoration to Christ, Whom the altar symbolizes, as St. Ambrose said. *"Christ"* means *"the Anointed One,"* and a church's altar is anointed with Sacred Chrism when the church is dedicated. We too, with the priest, must prepare

WE ENTER INTO THIS UNITY, THIS DEEP MYSTERY OF CHRIST AND THE CHURCH, FROM THE VERY MOMENT OF THE GREETING AT MASS.

the altar of our souls so that Christ may come to us. After each prayer, we say, *"Amen,"* which means we agree and believe!

The *Greeting* begins with the welcoming and with prayer. The priest leads us in making the Sign of the Cross. We call on the Holy

Trinity, Father, Son, and Holy Spirit, while remembering that Jesus died on the Cross not just to save us from our sin, which could have been accomplished in other ways, but to show the extent of His love for us. The priest invites the people to reflect on God's presence among us, saying *"The Lord be with you."*

"When Mass is being celebrated, the sanctuary is filled with countless angels who adore the divine victim immolated on the altar."

~St. John Chrysostom

We are members of the Christ's Church. He is our Head. We are His Body. When St. Augustine spoke of Christ united together with His Church, he called this unity *"the whole Christ."* We enter into this unity, this deep mystery of Christ and the Church, from the very moment of the *Greeting* at Mass. Let us be filled with joy and awe as we consider that the Lord is truly with us, and is present as our true Friend and our Redeemer!

CHAPTER 5

PENITENTIAL RITE

"*T*hose who are well do not need a physician, but the sick do*"* (cf. Mk 2:17). Christ's own words give us great peace and comfort. Jesus' very name means *"God saves."* He came to call a fallen world back to God. This is what He does at every Mass. The priest leads us in orienting ourselves more closely to God so that we can worthily participate in the rest of Mass. This involves seeking reconciliation with God and with one another, so that there is nothing keeping us from loving and being loved.

We want to be in the proper state of mind and soul to participate in the sacrifice and to receive Christ in Holy Communion.

We ask the Lord to forgive our faults that have offended Him, and He will do so. On the other hand, if we are aware of having committed a serious sin since our last Confession, we must first go to the Sacrament of Penance. We should still attend Mass, and participate fully but should not receive Communion until after we have received absolution in Confession. The Sacrament of Penance is the vehicle though which, like the Prodigal Son, we receive God's loving embrace again.

Before the Burning Bush, Moses took off his sandals because he was walking on holy ground before the Lord. A burning coal from Heaven's altar first purified Isaiah's lips so he could worthily proclaim God's Word. The Penitential Rite has those same elements. We acknowledge that we are not worthy of being in the presence of God and can approach Him only because of His grace given freely to us.

Through the waters of Baptism, we have been adopted into God's Family, the royal family of the universe. We recall these waters during Easter when the priest sprinkles the faithful with holy water at the beginning of the Mass as an act of penitence and purification.

We express our penitence to God and to each other, praying together: *"I confess to Almighty God and to you, my brothers and sisters..."* We say we are sorry to God together, and we apologize to our brothers and sisters in Christ for sometimes not giving the best example or for sinning against them. We promise to pray for each other, because we should always have our hearts open to reconcile with each other. We recall the two Great Commandments of Jesus: *Love God with your whole heart, soul, mind, and strength, and love your neighbor as yourself* (cf. Mt 22:37-39).

We are never closer to Heaven than when at Mass. We enter into communion with God and are in fellowship with the Blessed Virgin Mary and the saints and angels. Those who have already obtained the goal of eternal life are assisting us on our earthly journey to the finish line. They make up the Church in Heaven, redeemed men and women like us, who in Christ have achieved the victory of love!

14

CHAPTER 6

KYRIE ELEISON

When we ask God for forgiveness, we are asking Him for mercy. At this point in the Mass, we ask God's mercy three times, echoing the priest who is leading us. Asking three times shows sorrow for our sins, and symbolizes that we are praying to God as Father, Son, and Holy Spirit. Repetition is common in the psalms and in prayers at Mass. It helps to stir the heart, mind, and soul to prayer. As children often do, we too ask insistently for what we desire most: God's mercy and love. We pray together:

Lord, have mercy, Christ have Mercy, Lord have Mercy.

Much of the New Testament was written in Greek, and many of the early Christian liturgies were in Greek. Even though Latin became the language of the Roman Catholic Mass before the year 500, this prayer is still said in Greek, *"Kyrie eleison"* when it is not said in the vernacular. Christians have said this same prayer for over 1500 years!

In a mysterious act of love, God forgives us and accepts the debt to be paid by His Son, Who died on the Cross for us. What joy we feel that our debt has been paid! God sent His Son for us, and so we ask for mercy contritely, yet confidently, for His love and mercy are infinitely greater than our sins.

God loves us unconditionally. All He wants is for us to be in a relationship of friendship with Him, so, no matter what we have done, he wants us to go to Him. St. Therese of Lisieux spoke of herself saying *"... if I had committed all possible crimes, I would still have the same confidence. I would feel that this multitude of offenses would be like a drop of water cast into a blazing fire."* [1] It can be a challenge to our faith, to think of having a Father that wonderful, Who loves us to that degree. And yet, that is exactly Who the "Lord" and the "Christ" is in the *"Lord, have mercy"* prayer. We will see this theme of God's love and greatness reappear throughout the Mass.

St. Paul says, *"Where sin increased, grace overflowed all the more"* (cf. Rm 5:20). As we repeat the plea, "Lord, have mercy," we can never forget that our Father in Heaven is *"Rich in Mercy."*

Our confidence does not come from ourselves; instead, it comes from how great God is.

Thanks to saints like Saint Therese and St. Faustina, the Church is emphasizing greater appreciation of God's mercy in these times. But, it is something we need to think about even more in every Mass, as we implore God's mercy insistently and confidently. We focus on God's greatness and love, and a hymn of praise, thanks, and glory rises within our hearts! *Glory to God!*

[1] *Last Conversations, 89.*

CHAPTER 7

GLORIA

We make our own the hymn of the angels who sang to the shepherds announcing the Good News of the Birth of Jesus Christ: *"Glory to God in the Highest and on earth peace to people of good will!"* (cf. Lk 2:14). In this way, every mass is a renewal of Christmas; because it celebrates Christ's coming to us just as He came to the world over two thousand years ago.

The *Gloria* doxology (song of praise) was composed in the second century. Originally in Greek, it now forms part of the Mass in Latin from the 6th century. We sing out in thanks and praise to God for his greatness and love. The *Gloria* is always a hymn, sung or spoken, of the community, so everyone participates. In Advent and Lent, as a sign of penance, the *Gloria* is omitted. That is why on Christmas and Easter it returns often accompanied with joy and great celebration.

The *Gloria* is meant to externally express what our hearts are experiencing at this point in the Mass, and it leads our hearts to further joy. We wish to glorify God because of what He has done for us. We sing with joy, *"a great joy that will be for all the people"* (cf. Lk 2:10), as the angels said to the shepherds. We are humbled by the greatness of God, and in the middle of this prayer, *"Glory to God,"* we once again acknowledge that Jesus is the Source of mercy.

As the *Gloria* ends, we are reminded of the reason for our joy and our confidence: *"For you alone are the Holy One, You alone are the Lord, You alone are the Most High, Jesus Christ."* What joy to know that our Redeemer lives and He has restored us to life!

Christ's coming into the world is the historical climax of human history. All of history before Him was anticipating the Coming of the Messiah, and all of history after Him looks back to the moment when Jesus brought the gospel of salvation to the world; and in the Mass, this Event is recreated until the end of time. The *Gloria* is intoned at Christmas with bells rung out to celebrate the fulfillment of God's promise through the prophets: *"The people who walked in darkness have seen a great light; Upon those who dwelt in the land of gloom a light has shone"* (cf. Isaiah 9:2).

The experience of joy is similar during the Easter season. During, the rich symbolism of the Easter Vigil mass evokes our pilgrimage from darkness to light, from the grave of death to the sunrise of the Resurrection. In the Vigil mass, the Easter Candle enters the dark church, while the deacon chants, *"The Light of Christ!"* And then, at the *Gloria*, the church is flooded with light, symbolizing once a year what happens spiritually at this point in every Mass.

God has truly come to us. Christ is the proof of that. There is no brokenness we can ever experience that He cannot make whole.

And Christ comes to us, *"the only Son of the Father"* as a baby. He comes to us in the most humble, most accessible way. Who is threatened by a baby? Who isn't drawn to a newborn, and to wonder at the miracle of life? At this point in Mass, we too bow down, as the shepherds did entering the stable cave, to adore Jesus, praying aloud: *"We praise you, we bless you, we adore you, we glorify you, we give you thanks for your great glory!"*

The *Gloria* is one of the moments at Mass when we more easily see that Christ's life was one uninterrupted Revelation, a mission of God's love to save us. Christmas and Easter meet in the *Gloria*, the innocent Lamb of God embraces the wood of both cradle and cross.

THE GLORIA IS ALWAYS A HYMN, SUNG OR SPOKEN, OF THE COMMUNITY, SO EVERYONE PARTICIPATES.

CHAPTER 8

OPENING PRAYER

We come to Mass to pray together as members of Christ's Body, the Church. The priest solemnly invites us to pray the Opening Prayer, just before the readings that form the Liturgy of the Word. He pauses a moment so we can all unite our hearts in this prayer. All, together with the priest, observe a brief silence so that they may be conscious of the fact that they are in

God's presence and may offer the Mass for some personal intentions. Then the priest says the Prayer in which the spirit of the celebration is expressed – a new liturgical season, a memorial, a feast, or a Sunday solemnity.

In the early days of the Church in Rome, Christians would gather in one place and then walk together to a church for Mass. The Latin phrase *"plebs collecta"* – the people assembled – gave the *"Collect,"* the Opening Prayer, its name.

In the *"Collect"* the priest voices all our hopes and prayers for the Mass. Each day the Mass has a different Opening Prayer, and it often reflects the Scripture readings for that day. It is one of the parts of Mass that changes each day, and sometimes the priest has the option of choosing between several Opening Prayers in order to align the celebration more closely with local circumstances. The Prayer invites us to unite our hearts together as we all call upon our Father as His children. *"Catholic"* means universal, and during this Prayer, we think of and pray for all the Catholics throughout the world, who are united with us in celebrating the Mass that day!

"The Mass is the most perfect form of prayer!"
~Pope Paul VI

The Father, Son, and Holy Spirit are together called upon in the formal ending of this Prayer. By sharing His life with us, God has allowed us to be *collected*, gathered as a true universal family with Him in the Mass.

The Opening Prayer, since it changes every day, helps us to unite our prayers and sentiments to the Church calendar, also called the Liturgical Calendar or Liturgical Year. The Liturgical Year begins with the four weeks of Advent, which anticipates the Christmas Season. Then there is a brief period called "Ordinary Time" until Lent begins. The six weeks of Lent prepare us for Holy Week and Good Friday, which leads to the great celebration of Easter and the Easter Season, which lasts 50 days, ending with Pentecost and the Descent of the Holy Spirit. Then, "Ordinary Time" resumes until the yearlong cycle closes with the feast of Christ the King.

The Opening Prayer at Mass throughout the year has great variety and beauty. Saints such as Thomas Aquinas and Ignatius Loyola in fact wrote some of the Opening Prayers. In the course of the Church Year, our souls are led to consider all that God has done for us, and to pray for all the graces we need to make these wonderful mysteries fruitful in our lives. Throughout the year, we relive the Life, Death, and Resurrection of Christ. On memorial days we are also reminded of the virtues and examples of the saints.

THE PRAYER INVITES US TO UNITE OUR HEARTS TOGETHER AS WE ALL CALL UPON OUR FATHER AS HIS CHILDREN.

The great things that God has done for us are proclaimed in the words of Scripture. The Opening Prayer prepares our souls to listen to the Bible readings so that we will receive them like *"Seeds that have fallen on fertile ground"* (cf. Lk 8:8)

that will bear great fruit.

Think of all the Catholics throughout the world today. We all pray for the same thing each day in Mass. It is a wonderful expression of how *universal* our Faith is, beyond all boundaries of language, race, and border. Christ came to unite us in one family under the one Father. So we pray together as His Family, to the Father, through the Son, in the unity of the Holy Spirit.

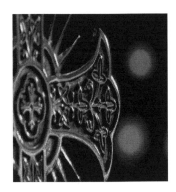

CHAPTER 9

LITURGY OF THE WORD

A s *prayer* characterizes the Introductory Rites, so now *listening* distinguishes the first of the two main parts of the Mass, the Liturgy of the Word. The word "liturgy" means a public service, a public duty.

As citizens of God's Kingdom, we have the privilege of listening to His Word, which is proclaimed at every Mass. We pray to be attentive to the Word and to allow the Word to transform us. The Word of God comes from the Holy Bible (Sacred

> AS CITIZENS OF GOD'S KINGDOM, WE HAVE THE PRIVILEGE OF LISTENING TO HIS WORD, WHICH IS PROCLAIMED AT EVERY MASS.

Scripture). The Word unites us as a people, as a family, to hear the wonders our God has done for us. Jesus speaks to us personally when we listen to the Readings with faith, attentiveness, and expectation.

As one of the reforms of the Mass after Vatican II, more readings were added to the Sunday Mass. Not an unprecedented addition, it hearkened back to an even earlier tradition, when the Readings from Scripture formed a more central role in the service. Typically, Sunday Mass contains a reading from the Old Testament, followed by the responsorial psalm, a reading from the New Testament (often from St. Paul's letters) and finally and most importantly, the Reading of the Gospel. Over the course of a three-year cycle, the Sunday Mass Readings go through most of the Bible, and all of the central themes of our Faith.

The Liturgy of the Word then continues with the homily by the priest, the Profession of Faith (also called the Creed) and the Prayers of the Faithful (petitions), where we place the needs of the community before God, confident in His love for us seen through the Readings.

The function of proclaiming the Readings is a ministry, a special service within the Church. Lectors typically read the first Readings, and a deacon or priest proclaims the Gospel.

Have patience with all things, but chiefly have patience with yourself. Do not lose courage in considering your own imperfections but instantly set about remedying them - every day begin the task anew.

~Saint Francis de Sales

THE CATHOLIC MASS...REVEALED!

CHAPTER 10

BIBLICAL READINGS

During the Liturgy of the word, we listen to God's Word speaking directly to us. St. Jerome famously said, *"Ignorance of Sacred Scripture is ignorance of Christ."* At Mass, we come to know Christ more personally and intimately through His Word.

The Mass, as we said, renews the Last Supper. But it is also the continuation of the traditions of God's Chosen People. Jesus Himself, when He visited the Synagogue of Nazareth, read out loud from the Prophet Isaiah (cf. Lk 4:16-20). He was showing us the importance of the Word for every age, every place, and every person. God truly speaks to each of us. He is the ultimate Author of the Bible, in which speaks to us through intermediaries, through those He inspired to write His Word, and at Mass through those who minister to us by reading and proclaiming His Word.

At Mass, the Bible Readings are organized into the Lectionary and the Book of the Gospels. Our grateful answer of *"Thanks be to God"* shows our openness to rise to the challenge of having been loved this much.

Through the Mass Readings, His Word prepares the Table of the Lord for us, and the riches of the Bible are opened to us[1] for fellowship with Him. We listen in silence as our souls absorb God's Word like a

timely rain. As Isaiah says, "...
*just as from the heavens the
rain and snow come down
and do not return there till
they have watered the earth,
making it fertile and fruitful, giving seed to him who
sows and bread to
him who eats, so shall
my word be that goes
forth from my mouth;
it shall not return to
me void, but shall do
my will, achieving the
end for which I sent
it"* (cf. Is 55:10-11).

WHILE IT IS ALWAYS
PROFITABLE FOR US TO READ
AND STUDY GOD'S WORD,
HEARING IT PROCLAIMED
IN MASS OFFERS SPECIAL
GRACES FOR US.

The Church teach-
es[2] us that Scripture
has two main senses or levels of understanding. First, there is the
literal meaning, which is what the human author is trying to com-
municate directly in what he is writing and where we see what God
has done for us, like freeing the Israelites from slavery in Egypt. The
second sense of Scripture as the Word of God is the spiritual sense,
which has three parts. The spiritual sense reveals the deeper meaning God intends for us to understand through the literal sense. The
spiritual sense can be either allegorical, when it is a sign of Christ
(like the Exodus prefiguring Christ's freeing us from sin), moral (see-

ing how Scripture is *speaking to us* about how to live a good and holy life), and what is called the "anagogical" spiritual sense, where the meaning sheds light on our eternal destiny (like how Jerusalem is a sign of the Church on earth and of the heavenly Jerusalem of the Church in Heaven).

While it is always profitable for us to read and study God's Word, hearing it proclaimed in Mass offers special graces for us. We are receiving it as God's assembled family, as a member of His Church where His Spirit dwells. All Catholics throughout the world are hearing these Readings today. Listening to our own spiritual family history, the story of our salvation through God's love, brings us closer to Christ and to each other.

[1]Vatican II, *Sacrosanctum Concilium*, 51.
[2]Cf Catechism of the Catholic Church 115-118.

CHAPTER 11

RESPONSORIAL PSALM

A family has its favorite stories. A family also has its favorite songs. God's family, the Church, has for many centuries also gathered each week to sing their favorite songs to God. The ancient family of Israel gathered in prayer each week on the Sabbath to listen to the Readings from the Old Testament. They would also

sing the songs of the Book of Psalms. So too, today we sing the Psalms in between the first two Readings each week at Sunday Mass (and recite one during the week). This adds Biblical richness to the Readings, and aids us in our meditation. Written mostly by King David, the Psalms are prayers and songs of variety, including of praise, petition, thanksgiving, with some historical and others prophetic. Just as they were put to music and sung in choir in Jerusalem centuries before Christ, the Psalms are also today sung at Sunday Mass, something Catholics have done since at least the third century or earlier.

The Psalms are so beautiful because we pray and sing the very prayers that the Lord has given us to pray from the Bible. Since the Lord is the primary Author of the Bible, the Psalms are the songs of the Lord, where God speaks to us. We sing and pray them to God as well. There are communities of monks who chant all 150 Psalms together each week, gathering up to seven times a day in the Liturgy of the Hours to worship God through the Divine Office. Like them, we are a worshipping community at Mass, and we too gather to pray the Psalms of the Lord in the middle of the "hour" of each Mass.

The Psalms usually include a refrain or psalm response that is a verse repeated several times as the Psalm is sung. The response is normally chosen to follow the theme of the Readings, and is meant to help us focus on a main theme of the Mass while in prayer. The Psalms lift our souls into all the heights and emotions of authentic prayer. With them, we sing out to God in joy, in wonder, in praise, but also when we are frightened, threatened, or weary because of the difficulties of the Christian life. The Psalms, like Christ, are divine in origin but also profoundly human. We see in them how much our Father in Heaven understands us and is close to us, helping us to pray and to draw near to Him. Singing the Psalms together helps the Word of God to be always upon our lips and in our hearts.

One cannot sing the Psalms and not think of David, the great

> THE PSALMS LIFT OUR SOULS INTO ALL THE HEIGHTS AND EMO-TIONS OF AUTHENTIC PRAYER. WITH THEM, WE SING OUT TO GOD IN JOY, IN WONDER, IN PRAISE, BUT ALSO WHEN WE ARE FRIGHTENED, THREATENED, OR WEARY BECAUSE OF THE DIFFICULTIES OF THE CHRISTIAN LIFE.

king of Israel in the Old Testament. He wrote many of the Psalms. We see that his life was in so many ways like our own. God chose him even though he was the least regarded of his brothers. David was tested and experienced struggle. He trusted in God as he faced insurmountable odds against the giant foe of Israel, Goliath, and he won victory. As a faithful servant of God, he endured persecution and jealousy. Though given many gifts from God, he was still a man with weaknesses and sins that he had to overcome with God's help and mercy. But he always repented, asking God for forgiveness, and returned to God with all his heart. God always forgave him. David writes about experiencing the forgiveness and mercy of God. He wanted to do great things for the Lord, and did with God's help! David had to struggle like any other father to guide his children on the right path. In his weaknesses, he would rely on the Lord, and the Lord in turn would bless him. It is from his descendants that Jesus was born. Through David and the Psalms, we learn that God can work wonders when we give ourselves to Him. God inspired David with the soul of a poet to write the Psalms that would be used by the Church at every Mass so many centuries later. These poetic prayers teach us that we too can pray in every circumstance of our lives, and God will help us today as He did David so long ago.

For prayer is nothing else than being on terms of friendship with God.

- Saint Teresa of Avila

Although written centuries before Christ, the Psalms speak of Him in prophetic ways, giving us details of His life and even how He would die.

In the Psalms, we find the roots of our faith. As prayers, the Psalms also teach us how to pray. They are the ideal source of Christian prayer. Priests and religious pray them each day, and do many lay Christians, in what is called the "Liturgy  of the Hours." So, at Mass, in the Responsorial Psalm we are accompanying all these people in the world, and Christ Himself, in the daily praying of the Psalms.

The Book of Psalms is the songbook of God's family, marking all the events of our life with God, our soul's greatest adventure.

THESE POETIC PRAYERS TEACH US THAT WE TOO CAN PRAY IN EVERY CIRCUMSTANCE OF OUR LIVES, AND GOD WILL HELP US TODAY AS HE DID DAVID SO LONG AGO.

CHAPTER 12

GOSPEL

The first four Books of the New Testament are called the Gospels. They were written by Sts. Matthew, Mark, Luke, and John, for whom they are named. The most important part of the Bible is the Gospel, because there we learn directly about Jesus Christ and His life. So, at Mass, the reading of the Gospel is the most important part of the Liturgy of the Word. We have heard what God inspired men to write in the Old Testament and in the Letters. Now, we listen to God's Own Son teaching us with His words and deeds, and by His life.

The reading of the Gospel is accompanied with great solemnity. It begins with the veneration of the Book by the priest or deacon. The Gospel Acclamation is then proclaimed. This is a verse pre-

ceded by the Hebrew word *"Alleluia"* (except in Lent), which means *"Praise God."* We should be attentive to the Acclamation and remember that the Bible says that the Word of God bears fruit with those who hear it and receive it with faith. Throughout the day, we should try to remember something we heard at Mass, especially from the Responsorial Psalm or Gospel Acclamation, so that it can make a lasting impression upon us and become a part of us.

THE MOST IMPORTANT PART OF THE BIBLE IS THE GOSPEL, BECAUSE THERE WE LEARN DIRECTLY ABOUT JESUS CHRIST AND HIS LIFE.

As we stand for the Gospel, we make three signs of the Cross with our thumb, one each on our head, our lips, and our heart, saying to ourselves: *Lord, be on my mind, on my lips, and on my heart forever.* This act helps us to remember that we want to understand God's Word, the Gospel, with our mind, share it with our lips, and love it with our hearts. We tell the Lord that we are here to listen and that we want Him to speak to our heart. We desire this not out of duty but for love. We ask the Holy Spirit to fill us with grace and understanding of the Gospel. We stand reverently to hear

the Gospel just as Rome's first Christ-ians did in the first century.

The Gospel Reading is the centerpiece of the first part of the Mass. The First Reading and the Opening and Closing Prayers are chosen to reflect and to shed light upon the Gospel's theme. Jesus who is the Word Incarnate, the Word Who became man, speaks to us most directly now through His Word in the Gospel. It is a Mystery of Faith, one that we can understand with faith. *The very same graces that Jesus gave to those who heard Him and saw Him while He was on earth, like in the Sermon on the Mount, are available to us now.* Just as He spoke to them, He is now speaking to us. The minister who reads the Gospel represents Christ to us, through his sharing in Christ's ministry as priest or deacon.

"In times past, God spoke in partial and various ways to our ancestors through the prophets; in these last days, he spoke to us through [his] son" (cf. Heb 1:1) The *Letter to the Hebrews* show us how important the Gospel is for us, both in Mass and in our lives. This is the divine Word of God, the same Word that created us, the Word that saved us, and the Word that will set us free. We accept

Christ as our Savior and our Lord, and what His Word teaches, with joyful worship when we say: *"Praise to you, Lord Jesus Christ!"*

The Sunday Mass Readings are designed in a cycle of three years. Three of the Gospel writers, Matthew, Mark, and Luke, are read once each year during Ordinary Time. And the fourth Gospel writer, John, is highlighted every year during Lent and Easter. On certain feasts, like Easter and Corpus Christi (The Body of Christ), a special poem is read, called the *sequence*, before the Alleluia verse, which prepares us to read the Gospel of the solemnity with greater emotion and depth.

The Gospel teaches us about Who Jesus is. It reveals His new law of love, which is not simply a code of conduct, but rather the following of a real Person, Who came down from Heaven to show us how to love, and to win for us the grace to live as children of the Father.

By reading and meditating on the Gospel passage, weekdays as well as on Sundays, we find the central Message God wants us to reflect upon and put into practice that day and all that week. His teaching is the light for our lives, which we are to put on the lampstand (cf. Mt 5:15) of our hearts and minds, to illuminate our house, our lives, and our world.

THIS IS THE DIVINE WORD OF GOD, THE SAME WORD THAT CREATED US, THE WORD THAT SAVED US, AND THE WORD THAT WILL SET US FREE.

CHAPTER 13

HOMILY

Because God loved us, He inspired the Scripture writers to write His words in the Bible. Because He loves us still, He inspires the bishops, priests, and deacons today to preach His Word at Mass, to help us apply it to our daily lives. This is one of the main purposes of the priesthood. The Sacrament of Holy Orders has three levels: deacons, priests, and bishops. All three levels share in the official teaching ministry of the Church. Though there are many forms of preaching, only ordained ministers preach homilies at Mass.

THIS HEART-TO-HEART TALK, OR HOMILY, NURTURES OUR CHRISTIAN LIFE AND GROWTH IN HOLINESS.

"Homily" comes from a Greek word meaning "conversation." In a family, our parents have conversations with us often, to teach us and nurture our growth. Priests, who are our spiritual fathers, also teach and converse with us about God's Word, including the Gospel, the Readings, and other aspects of the celebration at Mass including the theme of the liturgical calendar. This *heart-to-heart* talk, or Homily, nurtures our Christian life and growth in holiness. It gives us food for thought and opportunity for reflection. The Homily helps us to live the Mass in our lives and in our behavior throughout the whole week. It is not usually focused on the homilist himself or on his ingenuity and creativity of oration, but more on linking the readings themselves and on practical ways of putting the profound challenge of the Word into practice.

Christ Himself chose to spread His Kingdom mainly through

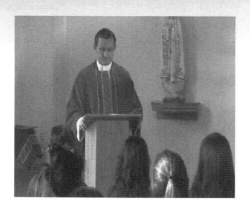

preaching. St. Paul teaches us that if people are to believe, they must first *hear* the Word preached to them (cf. Rom 10:14-15). God knows our needs so well, that He knows that we need to have, at least once a week, some words from a father-figure within our community, from someone who knows our lives and our struggles, and who has generously given his life in years of study and preparation, to guide us to understand and live the Gospel more deeply. This is the role of the priest; he represents Christ to us in the preaching of the Word and in the celebration of the Sacraments. Christ will always have something to say to us in every Homily if we listen with faith.

An important point of Catholicism is a wonderful interplay between what is universal and what is more particular or local. The Readings and Gospel being the same throughout the world at every Mass on every Sunday demonstrate this universal unity in the Mass. It is the same Mass and the same Word proclaimed everywhere in the world. In the Homily, the priest takes this *universal* Message of the Lord and applies it to the real lives of his local flock and parish, that is, to us.

As we prepare for the Eucharist, the Homily shows how the

one Word of God is applicable for the life of every person. In Saint Paul's words, *"All scripture is inspired by God, and useful for teaching, for refutation, for correction, and for training in righteousness, so that one who belongs to God may be competent, equipped for every good work."* (cf. 2 Tim 3:16-17) Through the Homily, the priest teaches us, sometimes correcting ideas or behaviors that need mending, and he also guides us to become better Christians.

CHRIST WILL ALWAYS HAVE SOMETHING TO SAY TO US IN EVERY HOMILY IF WE LISTEN WITH FAITH.

We all need to be competent in our faith, to be, as St. Peter says, *"ready to give an explanation to anyone who asks [us] for a reason for [our] hope"* (cf. 1Peter 3:15) The preacher at Mass also inspires us to be generous with our lives and focused on doing God's will, equipping us for service in His Name.

With our minds firm in faith and our wills inspired to live the Word with love, we can proceed with the Lord Jesus to His Table eager to receive strength for our journey, and all this through Him, with Him, and in Him Who is the Word made flesh.

CHAPTER 14

PROFESSION OF FAITH

O ur Faith is not just in a set of ideas; it is a belief and trust in the Person, Jesus Christ. Now, the priest leads us, as an assembly, to stand with dignity and profess our faith. In the Creed professed at Mass, we make a vocal affirmation of our faith in God.

From the beginning of Christianity, the Church has always handed on the Faith in brief formula doctrines for all to hold in common. The *Profession of Faith* summarizes the truths of the Faith and has three parts: first of the Father and creation, second of Christ and the work of Redemption, and third of the Holy Spirit and our sanctification. Called the *"Creed"* from the Latin word *Credo*, which means, *"I believe,"* it contains the twelve articles of belief that all baptized Catholics profess. Our

> THE PROFESSION OF FAITH SUMMARIZES THE TRUTHS OF THE FAITH AND HAS THREE PARTS.

profession is itself a prayer and not a rote recitation or mere repeating of doctrinal formulas.

There are several Professions of the Faith approved by the Church. The original and shorter *Apostles' Creed* was expanded by the Church's Ecumenical Councils of Nicea and Constantinople in the

4th century to correct various errors of belief present among some of the faithful at that time. Clarifying that Jesus was both human and divine, the *Nicene Creed* added, for example, and that Christ is *"God from God "* and  *"consubstantial with the Father."* The Nicene Creed was inserted into the Mass first at Antioch, and then in Rome, in the early centuries of Christianity. The most expansive official Profession of Faith of the Church is the *Credo of the People of God*, decreed at the end of the twentieth century by Pope Paul VI. All the Creeds of the Catholic Church agree with one another, and each is used in various ways today.

As we prepare to receive Christ in Holy Communion, we first express our *communion of belief* in the truths of Christ. As we begin the Creed together with the words, *"I believe,"* we are saying that we pledge ourselves to what we believe and to Christ Himself. As the hymn says: *"Faith of our Fathers, living still, in spite of dungeon, fire and sword, Oh how our hearts beat high with joy, whene'er we hear that glorious word!"*[1] The Creed is a prayer, one of the most important prayers of the Church. When we pray it with faith and proper disposition, the Holy Trinity comes to dwell in our souls. As we pray the Creed, we can reflect and thank those who struggled to hand on the Faith to us, from the Apostles and martyrs, to our own parents and friends. In praying the Creed together, we also renew our commitment to help each other grow in the Faith. The Father has created us, the Son has redeemed us, and the Holy Spirit is sanctifying us. This is the Good News that we must believe, live, and spread until Christ comes again!

All the articles of the Creed are rooted in the Gospel, and all the teachings of our Faith are linked to the Creed. *The Catechism of the Catholic Church*, the most authoritative text of the truths of the Faith, begins with an explanation of the Creed. We must *first* understand *what* God has revealed to us and done for us in the Creed, before we understand *how* we are invited to share in His love and grace in the Sacraments, particularly in the Eucharist at Mass.

> AS WE BEGIN THE CREED WITH THE WORDS, "WE BELIEVE," WE ARE SAYING THAT WE PLEDGE OURSELVES TO WHAT WE BELIEVE AND TO CHRIST HIMSELF.

The Creed and the Sacrament of Baptism are closely related. That is why occasionally at Mass, the rite of the renewal of Baptismal promises replaces the Creed as the Profession of Faith, like at a Mass that includes a Baptism. When we renew our Baptismal promises, we confirm that we reject what is against God and also confirm our belief in the fundamental truths of the Faith. It is moving to hear the priest say, *"This is our faith. This is the faith of the Church. We are proud to profess it, in Christ Jesus our Lord."*[2]

The Creed in the form of renewal of Baptismal promises has been

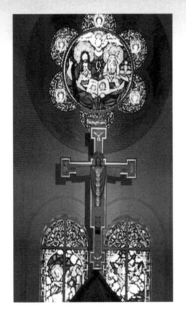

called the *"Sacramental Oath,"* and is a pre-requisite for Baptism. Each time we renew our Baptismal vows, we make a deeper commitment to live the life of grace and the life of Christ. When the *Catechism of the Catholic Church* was published, an emotional Cardinal embraced Pope John Paul II and said, *"This is the Faith I learned from my mother."* Professing our faith should move us; it should move us to greater love for Christ and His Church, and move us to be more active apostles in our world. This is *our* Faith!

EACH TIME WE RENEW OUR BAPTISMAL VOWS,
WE MAKE A DEEPER COMMITMENT TO LIVE THE LIFE
OF GRACE AND THE LIFE OF CHRIST.

[1]*Frederick W. Faber, Jesus and Mary (London: 1849); refrain by James G. Walton, 1874. (Faber studied at Oxford and was an Anglican clergyman who converted to Catholicism.)*
[2]*The Rite of Baptism*

THE CATHOLIC MASS...*REVEALED!*

CHAPTER 15

Prayer of the Faithful

After the Homily, we present our needs and petitions to God, whose loving goodness has just been revealed to us anew in Scripture. But, some have wondered why we need to ask God for anything, asking, *"Isn't He all-knowing?"*

Yes, God is all-knowing (Omniscient) and Jesus is God. Jesus understands all that is, in both His divine and human knowledge. But, while He knows all things, He told us that we must continually ask God, in faith, for what we need. For example, Jesus knew that wine was lacking at the Wedding at Cana, but He still waited for someone to notice and to ask Him before He worked the miracle. In this case, it was Our Lady her-  self who interceded for the newlyweds. At the Prayer of the Faithful, we follow Mary's example by inter- ceding for each other. We pray for the Pope, the Church and priests, for those in need, for peace, for sinners, for the sick, and the souls in Purgatory; we pray for everyone. We pray, *"Lord, hear our prayer."*

Our prayers of petition are necessary because God wants us to think about our needs and those of our neighbor, and then to acknowledge Who He is; and thus approach Him with love and

Three things are necessary for the salvation of man: to know what he ought to believe; to know what he ought to desire; and to know what he ought to do.

~Saint Thomas Aquinas
Two Precepts of Charity

confidence. The *Catechism* says, *"By prayer of petition we express awareness of our relationship with God. We are creatures who are not our own beginning, not the masters of adversity, not our own last end. We are sinners who as Christians know that we have turned away from our Father. Our petition is already a turning back to him."* [1]

"Conversion" means turning to God. And that is exactly what we do in the Prayer of the Faithful, also called the General Intercessions. As Peter said to Jesus, *"Master, to whom shall we go? You have the words of eternal life"* (cf. Jn 6:68). We too go to Jesus Who is all-knowing, all-powerful, and the source of eternal life.

As a result of Baptism, each of us shares in Christ's mission as priest, prophet, and king. We are a *royal kingly* people who reign through our service of others, as Jesus demonstrated by washing the Apostles' feet. We are *prophets* as we proclaim God's truth and profess our faith, to a world that does not know or even rejects Christ. And we exercise our *baptismal priesthood* at Mass through prayer and sacrifice for God's people. The Prayer of the Faithful is one important way we do this. The priest has a priesthood that is uniquely called "ordained ministry." He leads us in liturgical prayer and in the Consecration. At the Prayer of the Faithful, we unite with the priest and offer prayers to God for the salvation of all. The priest stands with us as we raise our petitions to God; as he represents God to us and intercedes for us to God.

Some scholars believe that the Prayer of the Faithful, in some form, was present in the liturgies of the first centuries, but fell out of use for a time. It was included after Vatican II and placed here at the end of the Liturgy of the Word. We respond to the Word of God with petitions to our Lord, which we pray together in faith.[2] God's love has already been revealed and explained to us, and so now we approach Him confident in His mercy, His power, and His infinite goodness.

The Mass is the celebration of our local parish family. But, it is not an event that is limited to one time and place. It is open to all peoples and cultures. It is as universal as the Faith itself, and as far-reaching as Christ Himself Who is the Savior of the world. We express this by praying for the whole Church and for the needs of the whole world. We pray for our specific local needs as well. Knowing that we need God and depend on Him for everything requires humility. But humility is nothing more than *"walking in the truth"* as St. Theresa of Avila says. The needs of the Church and the world are many. They are daunting. We can be tempted to throw up our hands, even to despair. But, we must have hope in Christ and call on Him in prayer for help, as the Church teaches: *"In the risen*

45

Christ the Church's petition is buoyed by hope, even if we still wait in a state of expectation and must be converted anew every day."[3] Every prayer is heard by Christ and answered for *our good* and for the good of those we pray for, even if it is not done so in our time and according to our ways.

"Lord, hear our prayer!" is the trusting petition of God's children who know how much He loves and cares for our *every* need.

[1] *Catechism of the Catholic Church, 2629.*
[2] *Cf. USCCB, General Instruction on the Roman Missal, n. 69.*
[3] *Catechism of the Catholic Church, 2630.*

CHAPTER 16

LITURGY OF THE EUCHARIST

T he first main part of the Mass was the Liturgy of the Word. The second main part of the Mass is the Liturgy of the Eucharist. Christ at the Last Supper established a Holy Sacrifice, and a banquet by which His Own Sacrifice on the Cross would be made present in the Church until the end of time.[1] During this time in the Mass, Christ Himself will soon descend upon the Altar through the Consecration Prayer.

For centuries this part of the Mass was reserved exclusively for Catholics in full communion with the Church, others would be dismissed. Catholics in the state of mortal sin who were still reconciling with the Church, (Penance was a lengthy and public process) were called the penitents, and non-Catholics in the process of joining the Church were called the catechumens. Both groups would be dismissed from the Mass after  the Liturgy of the Word to continue their process. Today, everyone is welcome at both parts of the Mass, though only those in full communion with the Catholic Church and who have the proper disposition may usually receive the Eucharist. Though all are welcome, in many places today, those preparing to become Catholics are still

dismissed after the Liturgy of the Word, as the faithful offer a prayer for them, to go and receive further instruction in the Faith nearby. They look forward with longing to the day when they will stay for the complete Mass, which will occur after they receive the Sacraments at the Easter Vigil.

In the Liturgy of the Eucharist, the priest, who represents Christ, fulfills Jesus' command at the last Supper to *"Do this in memory of Me."*

Each of the sections of the Liturgy of the Eucharist closely follows what Christ said and did at the Last Supper, just as He requested:

The *Offertory* and *Preparation of the Gifts* bring bread and wine to the Altar, just as Christ placed them upon His table with His Apostles.

The *Eucharistic Prayer* recalls and renews the prayer of Christ's thanksgiving for the Father's saving work while at the Last Supper. The bread and wine are consecrated and are changed into Christ's Body and Blood, Soul and Divinity during the Consecration, just as they were with Christ at the Last Supper.

THE CATHOLIC MASS...*REVEALED!*

Just as Christ took, blessed, broke, and distributed His Body and Blood at the Last Supper (the Four Great Eucharistic Acts), so too the priest does these four Eucharistic actions during the Liturgy of the Eucharist at Mass. And we receive Christ's Body and Blood, just as the Apostles did, in *Holy Communion*.

While the **externals** have varied much since Christ instituted the Mass at the Last Supper the night before He died two thousand years ago, the **essentials** have remained the same, and will until the end of time. The Liturgy of the Eucharist brings the moment of the Last Supper, the moment of Calvary and the Resurrection, and the moment of the Sacrifice of the Mass all together into a united Moment of grace. This is the greatest Event in the world and in history, *made present again* at every Mass.

St. John, who writes so much about what was said that night, tells us that Jesus *"loved his own in the world and he loved them to the end"* (Jn 13:1). In the Liturgy of the Eucharist, Christ calls us to touch and to experience the immense love that the Gospel talked about and prepared us for. Like the disciples on the road to Emmaus on the Day of the Resurrection, whose hearts were first burning within them as Jesus spoke His Word and then gave them His Eucharist, let us now come to experience this same Jesus!

¹*Cf. Vatican II, Sacrosanctum Concilium, 47.*

CHAPTER 17

PREPARATION OF THE GIFTS

A t Mass, we bring our gifts of bread and wine, our alms, and our very selves, to return enriched with the gifts of the Body and Blood of Christ and eternal life from God. The Fathers of the Church described Christ's Incarnation (when God became man) with the phrase *"admirable exchange"* that still forms part of the Christmas Mass prayer. The Mass truly is an *admirable exchange*! That is what the *Offertory* signifies at this part of the Mass. First we gather *(synaxis)* to prepare the Altar and then we make the offering *(anaphora)* of gifts to God.

In earlier times, the faithful brought their own bread and wine for the Sacrifice. Now, some of the faithful, representing all of us, bring the gifts of bread and wine to the Altar. The priest and altar serv-

ers prepare the Altar, which is the focal point of the Liturgy of the Eucharist. We present our gifts and tithes to God at this point, as we praise Him in song. The money we give shows that the first fruits of our daily work form part of our offering at the Mass. We offer our monetary gift to God through the Church, who will use the money for works of charity, for the poor, for the support of the priests, and for the Church's needs.

What we offer, then, is not merely something external. Our whole lives are an offering to God. Spiritually, we place our very selves upon the Altar with Christ as a gift to the Father. Like the bread and wine we brought forth

as the *"fruit of the vine and work of human hands,"* our lives are the result of God's gift and our own cooperation in work. We give the gifts of bread and wine to God now so that He can transform them into Christ Himself, so that the Eucharist can transform us into Christ, into other Christs. We will be nourished with Christ to continue His life in our world. We give what is human and receive what is divine… an *"admirable exchange"* indeed!

SPIRITUALLY, WE PLACE OUR VERY SELVES UPON THE ALTAR WITH CHRIST AS A GIFT TO THE FATHER.

We offer all that we are, all that we have, and all that we can. We place everything into the Hands of God. We experience what we offer being transformed as it is united to the Offering of Christ. We pray for our family, our friends, for our enemies, for those who asked for our prayers. We pray to lay down our lives on the Altar, with Christ on the Altar of the Cross, to be a blessing for those we pray for, to alleviate their sufferings and problems. We say with St. Paul in Scripture, *"I have been crucified with Christ"* (Gal 2:20). *Blessed be*

When we have been to Holy Communion, the balm of love envelops the soul as the flower envelops the bee.

~Saint Jean Vianney

God forever!

To *"consecrate"* something means to set it apart. Sunday is a whole day that is consecrated to God; it is set apart for God and is thus special. It is set apart for worshipping God, for prayer, for rest, for works of mercy, and for family time. The gifts that we bring to the Altar are set apart for God. They will soon be consecrated in a special way to God.

As Jesus changed the water into wine during the wedding at Cana, the bread and wine will now be transformed into the Body and Blood of Christ by the Consecration of the Mass. We pray that our lives will be transformed as well. As the priest prepares the gifts, he pours a drop of water into the wine and says, *"By the mystery of this water and wine, may we come to share in the divinity of Christ, who humbled Himself to share in our humanity."* The water represents the little we offer to the wine that God uses to bless us. We do so little and Christ does so much, but the little we do is important too. We are preparing to be united in communion with Christ like the water into the wine. This, most importantly, is why we come to Mass.

Through our Baptismal consecration, we have been set apart for God. He placed the seal of His love upon us. We belong to Him.

Before this, our own sinfulness had in a sense *"owned"* us. We were slaves of sin and death even through Original Sin, but now we are free people of grace and life. Christ paid the price for us by redeeming us. To *"redeem"* means to buy back. He purchased our freedom for us. And the price was His Own Blood. Like the father of the prodigal son in Jesus' parable, God doesn't accept us back as servants, but fully as His sons and daughters, as co-heirs with our Brother Christ in the Heavenly Kingdom.

THROUGH OUR BAPTISMAL CONSECRATION, WE HAVE BEEN SET APART FOR GOD. HE PLACED THE SEAL OF HIS LOVE UPON US.

This awesome mystery of our littleness and God's greatness is symbolized and made real in the Preparation of the Gifts. Our hearts cry out like the Psalmist: *"How can I repay the Lord for all the good done for me?"* And, with him, our hearts respond: *"I will raise the cup of salvation and call on the name of the Lord. I will pay my vows to the Lord in the presence of all his people"* (cf. Ps 116:12-14).

CHAPTER 18

PRAYER OVER THE OFFERINGS

Because God loves us, He sent His Son to die on the Cross for us. Because He loves us still, He sends His Son to become our spiritual Food in the Eucharist. As the gifts are prepared and the Eucharistic Prayer approaches, we are invited to deepen our prayer. The priest says, *"Pray, brethren, that my sacrifice and yours may be acceptable to God..."* The priest offers the Sacrifice with us and for us. We pray together that God receive our gifts, which we have offered with sincerity of heart.

The First Eucharistic Prayer recalls the long tradition in Scripture of offering sacrifices to God: *"the gifts of your servant Abel the just, the sacrifice of Abraham, our father in faith, and the offering of your high priest Melchizedek."* We pray that we lead lives worthy of these offerings. Our relationship with God is based on what we receive from Him and what we give Him in return. Love thrives through giving and receiving. God made us; He redeemed us, He blesses and sanctifies us; He takes care of us and  all our needs, temporal and spiritual; He hears our prayers and answers us for our good. We show our love to God by offering Him sacrifice. We give a sign of our love through offering bread and wine, and our alms. We also give our petitions, our concerns, our hopes, our sufferings, our trials, our relaxations, our very lives to Him, united with Christ on the Altar, to the eternal Father.

For the second time at Mass, the priest invites us to prayer. This short "Prayer over the Gifts" is another prayer, like the Opening Prayer, which changes each Sunday. It connects the different times of the Church Year to this central part of the Mass: offering all we are and have to God, including Christ's Self-offering to the Father for our Redemption.

THIS PRAYER, LIKE THE JEWISH TABLE BLESSING IT ORIGINATES FROM, SHOWS THAT WE ARE TO THANK GOD FOR ALL CREATION.

When we say (or sing) *"Amen"* to this prayer, we are declaring that we are accepting Christ's invitation to His banquet. And we pray, *"May the Lord accept the sacrifice…"*

When we pray before a meal, we thank God for what we have to eat, and ask Him that it be for our health and benefit. Similarly, at Mass when the priest prays over the gifts, the he says, *"Blessed are You, Lord, God of all creation…"* This prayer, like the Jewish table blessing it originates from, shows that we are to thank God for all creation. He gives us all good things so that we might know Him, love Him, and serve Him in a relationship of love.

The Prayer over the Offerings used to be called the "Secret" because the priest pronounced it in a whisper. In fact, the whole Eucharistic Prayer was once whispered, since it was seen as a priestly prayer. Now it is said aloud so that we too can participate. The priest prays "in Persona Christi", and we join our own prayers to the one sacrifice of Christ. Christ's priests serve us in many ways, and are essential to our life in Christ, as they consecrate the Eucharist, preach the Word, baptize our children, and reconcile us to Christ and the Church from cradle to grave. We can thank God for the priests at this point in the Mass.

Before Christ offered His Sacrifice, before He gave His Apostles His Body and Blood to eat, He first washed their feet, an act of extremely humble service. His ultimate act of service was giving His very life for us, and then continuing this Offering in the Eucharist until the end of time, so He could be with us always.

Christ then said, *"Do you realize what I have done for you? I have given you a model to follow, so that as I have done for you, you should also do."* (cf. Jn 13: 12, 15) St. John shows us what our attitude should be at Mass. As we offer ourselves to God, we also offer ourselves to each other in love and service. Only in this way can we follow Christ who *"did not come to be served but to serve and to give his life as a ransom for many."* (cf. Mt 20:28) We are called to offer our lives, especially our sufferings, for those in need, united with Christ as redemptive suffering.

CHAPTER 19

EUCHARISTIC PRAYER—PREFACE

The Eucharist is the source, summit, and font of the Christian life.[1] The Eucharistic Prayer is therefore the center and summit of the Mass and of all the Church's prayer. The Mass is the prayer of prayers and at its heart is the Liturgy of the Eucharist. The beginning of the Eucharistic Prayer, called the *Preface*, centers our attention on what we are about to do. The priest once again makes us aware of God's presence among us, saying *"The Lord be with you."* With arms outstretched he exhorts us to *"Lift up your hearts,"* and then says, *"Let us give thanks to the Lord, Our God."* After asking for God's mercy at the beginning of Mass, and hearing God's truth in His Word, our hearts overflow with thanks as we approach the Eucharistic Prayer. After all, *"Eucharist"* comes from the Greek word for *giving thanks*. In the Preface, led by the priest, we thank God for His work of salvation in adoration and obedience.

In the Roman Rite, there are many different Preface prayers used as options depending on the Liturgical Season, the Feast Day or Saint's day. In each one, we thank God for that part of His masterful mosaic seen in the event or the Saint we are remembering. These Preface prayers are beautiful prayers which can help us delve deeper into the mysteries of Christ and participate better in the Consecration.

Above all, we thank God for sharing His life with us through grace.

We, who could only hope to be His servants, have been made His children, thanks to the Sacrifice of His Son. As St. John writes, *"See what love the Father has bestowed on us that we may be called the children of God. Yet so we are."* (cf. 1 Jn 3:1) As His children, we discover that our whole sacrifice given to God at Mass has been returned to us transformed, sanctified and blessed by Him.

IF WE ARE FAITHFUL TO HIS GRACE, WE WILL BE HAPPY WITH HIM IN THIS LIFE AND FOREVER IN HEAVEN.

If we are faithful to His grace, we will be happy with Him in this life and forever in Heaven. The Preface ends with great solemnity and with yet another reminder that our Mass is a participation in the eternal celebration of communion taking place in Heaven.

[1] *Cf. Vatican II, Lumen Gentium, #11; cf. Catechism of the Catholic Church, #1324.*

CHAPTER 20

EUCHARISTIC PRAYER—ACCLAMATION

As we thank God for His saving work, we also recall that our prayer is in Christ and in His Holy Name. *"Jesus"* means *"God saves"*. As the Angels praised Him at His birth, which we echo in the *Gloria*, we now join them again in their heavenly acclamation taken from Isaiah's vision of God on the throne of his Temple (cf. Is 6:1-3). The priest, choir, and congregation sing out: *"Sanctus, Sanctus, Sanctus – Holy, Holy, Holy!"*

This hymn is among the most ancient in the Mass. It has been part of the Mass since Pope St. Sixtus in the second century, and even the Latin version contains some words from Hebrew, showing a continuity of worship between the Old and New Testament prayers. We call God *"Dominus Sabaoth"* or *"Lord of Hosts,"* and we use the Hebrew acclamation of praise: *"Hosanna!"*

We prayed in the Creed to God the Creator *"of all that is seen and unseen"*. We echo that again here in prayer, praising God for Heaven, for creation unseen, and for the visible realm of earth, which are all *"full of his glory."* His glories, as Isaiah saw, fill Heaven His throne and earth His footstool.

As we say, *"Blessed is He who comes in the name of the Lord,"* we are using the words of those who waved palm branches as Jesus entered Jerusalem a few days before His crucifixion. (cf. Mk 11:9). The *"glory in the highest"* of Christmas becomes here the *"Hosanna*

The celebration of Holy Mass is as valuable as the death of Jesus on the cross.

~ *Saint Thomas Aquinas*

in the highest" of Palm Sunday.

Yet, we remember as well that the praises of Palm Sunday will soon change to shouts of *"Crucify Him!"* five days later. The Lord understands that our praise is often weak, that our sincerity can be inconstant. As He entered Jerusalem and received the praises due to Him, He knew as well that He would soon die by those who praised Him.

As we sing the *Sanctus*, we acclaim the Triune God as three-times *holy*. While so far greater than us, in Christ He will give Himself to us, and elevate us unto Himself, making us holy like He is holy. And we now relive that Offering of Christ for us on the Altar of the Cross and of the Mass. At the priest's invitation, we all unite in the hymn of the Angels, singing the *Sanctus*, a prayer of praise, with its exclamation of *Hosanna*, in which we beg the Lord to save us. The Liturgy is now approaching its summit. We sometimes stand for prayer, and that custom is followed in many parts of the world even for the Eucharistic Prayer. Since kneeling is the common posture for prayer in the United States, the bishops have obtained approval for us to follow that custom in the great Eucharistic Prayer.

You can imagine the thousands of Angels and Saints who are present, praying in reverence, and the many angelic choirs singing in unison together with the faithful: *Holy, Holy, Holy!* St. John Chrysostom observed this reality saying, *"The whole sanctuary and the space before the altar is filled with the heavenly Powers come to honor Him who is present upon the altar."* You can imagine the

THE CATHOLIC MASS...*REVEALED!*

multitude of Saints, full of joy as they arrive and join the Angels in singing to God. You can imagine Our Lady, who is standing a little behind the priest. You imagine all the heavenly participants as the Consecration begins. And you can imagine the souls in Purgatory, who are awaiting your prayers for them (since they cannot pray for themselves), to refresh them and help them to receive merit from the Mass and thus get to Heaven sooner. What an incredible reality, the Church Triumphant, the Church Suffering, and the Church on

Earth united together with the Lord God at every Mass! No wonder the venerable Cardinal Newman said, *"To me nothing is so consoling, so piercing, so thrilling, so overcoming, as the Mass... it is a great action, the greatest action that can be on earth."* The Mass, where space and time suspend, Heaven and Earth Unite!

CHAPTER 21

EUCHARISTIC PRAYER—INVOCATION

After praising God's power, we now call upon it. Christ is about to become present upon the Altar, hidden under the form of bread and wine. In Nazareth, Our Lady was told that God's Son would become present within her, His divinity hidden under the form of an unborn child. The Angel explained to her, *"The Holy Spirit will come upon you, and the power of the Most High will overshadow you"* (cf. Lk 1:35). Christ's presence on earth required God's power, though He willed that Mary's collaboration, her *"yes"*, also would be needed. Faith in God does not exclude the need for His people to cooperate with their part, as Mary exemplifies. Throughout the Mass, we too have given our *"yes"* to God, expressed our willingness to receive Christ into our hearts, into our lives, and through us into our world.

At this point of the Eucharistic Prayer, we pray for the presence of God in a special way. He is already present in the congregation, as He promised that He would be present whenever two or three persons are gathered in His Name (cf. Matt 18:20), through the Word proclaimed and preached, and through the priest; and now we call upon the Holy Spirit to come upon the gifts we bring, and transform them into His Real Presence.

Although the Mass has been celebrated from the beginning of the Church by the Apostles, some of its prayers have changed from time to time in the Church's history. The first Eucharistic Prayer is called the Roman Canon. It is the most ancient in the Roman Church, dating from the sixth century in much like its present form. It was the only Prayer used by the Roman Church until after Vatican II. The other Eucharistic Prayers are based on Greek and other liturgies,

some dating from the second century. The Eucharistic Prayers begin by calling upon God's power before the Consecration. It is at this moment that the priest extends his hands over the offerings in prayer.

To call upon is to invoke. The technical term for this moment of the Eucharistic Prayer is the *"epiclesis,"* a Greek word meaning *"invocation."* We invoke God's power for the offerings to be consecrated and transformed into Christ's Body and Blood, and we invoke His power that we who will receive Him in Communion may likewise be transformed into Him.

God's *"fiat,"* *"let there be…,"* created the universe at the beginning of time. Mary's *"fiat,"* *"let it be done unto me,"* brought forth the Redeemer of the universe two thousand years ago. As we invoke the Holy Spirit at this part of the Mass, let us prepare to embrace the miracle of Christ's presence by likewise saying *"yes"* with our whole lives.

CHAPTER 22

EUCHARISTIC PRAYER—INSTITUTION NARRATIVE

Jesus Christ came into this world to bring all mankind back to the Father. His whole life, from his Incarnation through his Resurrection, is geared toward our Redemption. At Mass, the culminating moment comes now, when the priest repeats Jesus' very words and gestures at the Last Supper. The priest carries forward the priesthood Jesus instituted that first Holy Thursday night. The priest acts in *Persona Christi*, *"in the Person of Christ,"* as he consecrates the Eucharist. Christ is both the Priest and the Victim of Sacrifice.

This part of the Eucharistic Prayer is called the Institution Narrative because it recalls when and how Christ instituted the

Eucharist, and with it, His holy priesthood. *"On the night He was betrayed…"* Jesus knew well that some of His followers throughout time would reject the fruits of His Sacrifice and His teaching on His Presence in the Eucharist. His actions are direct and clear, His words simple and straightforward. But, He knew some would not believe and would even leave Him. This is foreshadowed at the end of His discourse on the Eucharist, in John chapter 6, when some of His disciples will no longer follow Him because they do not believe He will give us His flesh to eat and His Blood to drink.

At this part of every Mass throughout the world, Christ comes again into the world, to renew His Sacrifice, although in an unbloody manner, upon the Altar. The Church offers us various gestures and signs to help us consciously recognize and fruitfully make a solemn act of Faith in Christ's Real Sacramental Presence: the tolling of bells... the lighting of a candle... the rising of incense... and the elevation of the Body and Blood.

The bread and wine are consecrated separately because that is what Jesus did at the Last Supper. However, the Church believes and teaches that He is fully present in both the host and the chalice. The resurrected and glorified Christ cannot be divided. The Eucharist is Christ, Body and Blood, Soul and Divinity.

The consummation of the Eucharistic Sacrifice is at the same time the ultimate proof of the power of His love. *"No one has greater love than this, to lay down one's life for one's friends."* (cf. Jn 15:13) Jesus gives Himself totally for us to the Father in the Sacrifice and totally to us in Holy Communion, and further earns for us the grace to be called His friends. His Hands once outstretched and nailed to the Cross in history are now represented and extended to us at Mass in the greatest act of love and friendship.

CHAPTER 23

EUCHARISTIC PRAYER—ELEVATION

WE ARE WITH JESUS AT HIS TABLE AND AT THE FOOT OF HIS CROSS AS THE PRIEST ELEVATES THE SACRED HOST AND CHALICE.

Jesus instituted the Eucharist at the Last Supper as the New Covenant in His Blood. In the Old Testament, covenants between God and His people were ratified through a bloody sacrifice. Moses sprinkled the people with blood as a sign of their acceptance of the covenant of Sinai (Ex 24:8). Holding the victim up in this way made the community share in the sacrificial duties of the priest. The Mass is the Sacrifice of the New Covenant. The Holy Sacrifice of the Mass *"completes and surpasses all the sacrifices of the Old Covenant"* (Catechism #1330). At Mass, Holy Thursday unites with Good Friday. We are with Jesus at His table and at the foot of His Cross as the priest elevates the Sacred Host and Chalice. And our prayers are strongest at the Consecration in Holy Mass, during the Elevation of the Host and Chalice.

As the priest genuflects in profound adoration, our souls also bow down before the Divine Majesty, now present on the Altar, and the majesty of Christ's love, poured out for us in His Body and Blood. We recall the words of St. Thomas Aquinas: *"Blood that but one drop of has the power to win all the world forgiveness of its world of sin."*

Jesus said *"when I am lifted up from the earth, I will draw every-*

one to myself" (cf. Jn 12:32.) He was lifted up on the Cross, but is also lifted up at every Mass.

As the Host is raised, we can make an act of faith, like St. Thomas the Apostle, who at first doubted but came to believe, saying *"My Lord and My God"* (cf. Jn 20:28). We may also adore the Lord silently saying, in the words of St. Francis, *"My God and my All."* As the Chalice is elevated, we can renew our Covenant with the Lord, and appreciate the forgiveness it brings us, saying, *"My Jesus, Mercy!"* in the silence of our soul in adoration. In this moment, we can look upon the Lord and contemplate Him, exchanging gazes, and pray: *"Lord, I believe, I adore, I trust and I love You. I ask pardon for those who do not believe, do not adore, do not trust, and do not love You."* Tell Jesus how much you love Him.

There is nothing so great as the Eucharist. If God had something more precious, He would have given it to us.

~ *Saint Jean Vianney*

CHAPTER 24

TRANSUBSTANTIATION— MIRACLE OF MIRACLES

"*This is the bread that comes down from heaven so that one may eat it and not die. I am the living bread that came down from heaven; whoever eats this bread will live forever; and the bread that I will give is my flesh for the life of the world.*" (cf. John 6:50-51)

"*Unless you eat the flesh of the Son of Man and drink his blood you have no life in you … he who eats my flesh and drinks my blood abides in me and I in him*" (cf. John 6:53-56). These are the words of Christ and present us with an awesome truth. But how can we even begin to understand them?

St. Thomas Aquinas tried to explain it by using the philosophical

terms identified by the Greek philosopher Aristotle[1]. There are two key elements: substance and accident. For Aquinas (and Aristotle), "substance" is the quality that makes a particular thing be that thing. For example, the reality that makes a piece of wood be wood. All wood is wood, even though different pieces may have different shapes, different colors, and different hardness. It is still wood. The quality that makes it "wood" is called "substance." The differences between the various woods are called "accidents." They are not essential to the reality that underlies them.

Applying those principles to the consecration of the bread and wine, St. Thomas explains that here the *accidents*, the **external appearances**[2], the color, smell, even the taste of bread and wine, all remain. But the *"what it is,"* the *substance*, changes. *It* **is** no longer bread, but **is** the Body and Blood of Christ, now under the appearance (what theologians call the *"sacramental species"*) of bread and wine.

When we receive Holy Communion, we experience something extraordinary - a joy, a fragrance, a well being that thrills the whole body and causes it to exalt.

~ Saint Jean Vianney

During Christ's life, his divinity was veiled through his human nature. It was his humanity that was apparent to us. To believe He was God required an act of faith. Now, in the Eucharist, both Christ's divinity and humanity are hidden, veiled by the sacramental species. It requires a great act of faith to say that what appears to us as bread and wine is the Body of Christ. But we take Jesus at his word when he said at the Last Supper: *"This **IS** my body....this **IS** my blood."*

This unique and miraculous act, by which something changes its *substance* while its *accidents* remain, is called "transubstantiation." The Council of Trent (1551) officially incorporated the term in its definitive teaching on the Eucharist, by stating: *"By the consecration of the bread and wine there takes place a change of the whole substance of the bread into the substance of the body of Christ our*

Lord and of the whole substance of the wine into the substance of his blood. This change the holy Catholic Church has fittingly and properly called transubstantiation." Since all that is required is faith, even young children can understand that this is not bread, but Christ himself, as the *"Bread of Life"*. For this reason St. Pius X lowered the age of reception of Holy Communion to the age of reason (seven or eight years of age), and encouraged the frequent reception of Communion.

THIS UNIQUE AND MIRACULOUS ACT, BY WHICH SOMETHING CHANGES ITS SUBSTANCE WHILE ITS ACCIDENTS REMAIN, IS CALLED "TRANSUBSTANTIATION."

[1]*"It seems", said Aristotle, "that there are two basic ways for something to exist. Something can exist in itself, like a dog or a tree or a person, or it can exist in something else, like the color red or the quantity two or an action like throwing. You don't ever see red, but something red, you count two only in relation to two things; there is no throwing if something or someone isn't doing it".*
[2]*These accidents are also called "species" by philosophers, --employing a different sense of the word than when used by biologists.*

CHAPTER 25

EUCHARISTIC PRAYER—
IN MEMORY OF HIM

The words of Consecration end with Christ's command, *"Do this in memory of me"* (cf. Lk 22:19). Our Mass makes His Sacrifice a reality on the altar. After the Elevation of the Host and Chalice, we proclaim the *mystery of faith*. On the Altar now is Jesus resurrected. What was bread and wine is now the real person of Jesus, body and blood, soul and divinity, in everything except physical appearance. A miracle has happened - the Miracle of all miracles!

"Mystery" comes from the Greek word that is translated into Latin as *"sacramentum"* or sacrament. The *"mystery of faith"* that we proclaim is not just the truth we say, it is the Eucharist! We make an act of faith together, proclaiming that the Eucharist before us is Christ, who died, rose from the dead, and will come again as He promised. He is already *come again* in a certain sense in the Eucharist.

The next section of the Eucharistic Prayer is called the *"anamnesis,"* another Greek word, meaning *"remembrance."* Here we call to mind all that Christ has done for us, recalling especially His Passion, Death, Resurrection, and Ascension into Heaven. We remember as well that Christ will come again in glory at the end of time.

Christ came first as a baby in Bethlehem. He will come again glorious and triumphant at the end of time, just as He left at the Ascension. But He also comes to us each day of our lives, especially in the Eucharist. Remembering all that Christ is and has done nourishes our faith and fills us with joy.

CHAPTER 26

EUCHARISTIC PRAYER—OFFERING

Our prayer is directed to the Father, through the Son, in the Holy Spirit. The Eucharistic Prayer is no exception, and in it we explicitly offer Christ as a spotless Victim to the Father, in the Holy Spirit. All prayers, all other offerings, lead up to this Offering of the Mass. There is no prayer more perfect, no offering more acceptable to God than His Own Son.

ALL PRAYERS, ALL OTHER OFFERINGS, LEAD UP TO THIS OFFERING OF THE MASS.

In the first Eucharistic Prayer, the Roman Canon, the priest recalls the gifts of Abel, the sacrifice of Abraham, and the bread and wine offered by Melchizedek. St. Irenaeus compared this Old Testament foreshadowing to the Gospel parable of the field with the hidden treasure[1]. The treasure is Christ, and all prior sacrifices of the old covenant find their perfection and fulfillment in Christ's Sacrifice in the Mass. What joy is ours since we have discovered this treasure!

The Church offers Christ to the Father at every Mass, and through the priest's words we also offer ourselves, united with Christ. All of the prayers and our whole lives, with all our imperfections, find their perfection and fulfillment when united to Jesus as our joint offering to the Father. Our whole life becomes part of this offering of love, as the traditional Morning Offering Prayer acknowledges with such beautiful words, *"I offer You my prayers, works, joys, and sufferings of this day."* We then pray in a way that gives our lives immeasurably increased value by combining them with the infinite value of the Mass, stating that they are offered *"in union with the Holy Sacrifice of the Mass offered throughout the world."*

OUR WHOLE LIVES ARE THUS UNITED WITH THE OFFERING OF CHRIST AT EVERY MASS.

Our whole lives are thus united with the Offering of Christ at every Mass. The Eucharist is the source and summit of the Christian life and *of each Christian's life.* We pray that our lives will be brought to completion through Christ into unity with God by the Holy Spirit, and with each other, so that, as St. Paul prayed, *"God may be all in all"* (cf. 1 Cor 15:28).

It would be easier for the world to survive without the sun than to do without Holy Mass.

~ *St. Pio of Pietrelcina (Padre Pio), stigmatic priest*

[1] *Cf. St. Irenaeus, Against Heresies, Book 4, Chapter 26.*

CHAPTER 27

EUCHARISTIC PRAYER—INTERCESSIONS

St. Paul reminded St. Timothy, *"For there is one God, and there is one mediator between God and men, the man Christ Jesus"* (1 Tim 2:5). Christ is our Mediator, interceding for us before the Father and representing Him to us. Priests in many ways further mediate Christ to us, and they represent Christ for us. Through their priesthood *"Christ unceasingly builds up and leads his Church."*[1] The Pope is the Supreme Pontiff of the Church of Christ. The word *"pontiff"* comes from the Latin word *"Pontifex,"* meaning *"bridge builder."* The Pope and the priests pray for us continually, especially at Mass, and we also pray and intercede for each other with them.

CHRIST IS OUR MEDIATOR, INTERCEDING FOR US BEFORE THE FATHER AND REPRESENTING HIM TO US.

We celebrate the Eucharist in communion with the whole Church, both in Heaven and on earth. Thus, we pray for the whole Church in the Eucharistic Prayer. The Prayer mentions the Pope by name, the Shepherd of the universal Church. In this Prayer, we also pray for our diocese and our bishop by name, because he is the shepherd of our local church. We pray for all members of the Church, those living as well as those who have passed away and may need our prayers in Purgatory. After

THE POPE AND THE
PRIESTS PRAY FOR
US CONTINUALLY,
ESPECIALLY AT MASS,
AND WE ALSO PRAY AND
INTERCEDE FOR EACH
OTHER WITH THEM.

embracing the whole world and the Church in these intercessions, the focus is once again brought back to the Altar, where Christ is present *"through whom [the Father] bestow[s] on the world all that is good."*

What we pray for is as significant as *for whom* we pray. As we offer Christ's one Sacrifice, we pray that the fruits and benefits of this Sacrifice may reach the whole world, for we all have been called to participate in the redemption and the salvation purchased by Christ's Body and Blood. These prayers of intercession in the Eucharistic Prayer are extremely beautiful and exemplify the commandment to love our neighbor.

[1]*Catechism of the Catholic Church, 1547.*

CHAPTER 28

EUCHARISTIC PRAYER—GREAT AMEN

The Eucharistic Prayer ends reminding us of the purpose for the Mass, indeed the purpose for everything: *God's glory*. As baptized Christians who share God's life in grace, we give glory to God through Christ, with Christ, and in Christ.

At this point the priest holds the Eucharistic Christ aloft once again, raising the Host and the Chalice slightly, in an act which dates back to the early Church, called the

The heavens open and multitudes of angels come to assist in the Holy Sacrifice of the Mass.

~ Saint Gregory

"*Little Elevation*," to distinguish it from the greater elevations at the Consecration, which date from the middle Ages. The Sacrifice has now been consummated. The bread and wine, which have been changed

into Christ's Own Body and Blood, have been presented to God the Father. We pray to God that all glory be given to Him through Christ, the Christ Whom the priest holds in his hands, who became man for us, died for us and in an infinite outpouring of love is now coming to us!

At the end of the Eucharistic Prayer, the faithful declare their assent to the prayers of the priest in the *Great Amen*. We have seen that the Mass contains elements of Latin, Greek and even Hebrew. Now, the language Jesus Himself spoke with His disciples has its most

AT THE END OF THE EUCHARISTIC PRAYER, THE FAITHFUL DECLARE THEIR ASSENT TO THE PRAYERS OF THE PRIEST IN THE GREAT AMEN.

solemn expression. *"Amen"* is Aramaic, and means *"so be it"*, or more simply *"truth"* or *"yes"*. The *"Amen"* that closes the Eucharistic Prayer is called the *"Great Amen"* because we say *"yes"* to all that the Eucharistic Prayer has expressed. We offer our *yes* to God to thank Him for His faithfulness, and to pledge our trust in Him, to promise to live our lives for His glory, as we had just prayed. The *Catechism of the Catholic Church* states beautifully, *"Jesus Christ himself is the 'Amen.' He is the definitive 'Amen' of the Father's love for us. He takes up and completes our 'Amen' to the Father: 'For all the promises of God find their Yes in him. That is why we utter the Amen through him, to the glory of God.'"*[1]

[1] *Catechism of the Catholic Church*, 1065.

CHAPTER 29

LORD'S PRAYER

After the Eucharistic Prayer, with Christ's Real Presence on the Altar, the Mass now focuses on preparing us to receive Jesus in Holy Communion. This part of the Mass – the Lord's Prayer, the Rite of Peace and the Lamb of God, together with the reception of Holy Communion – all form part of what is called the *"Communion Rite."* We enter the climatic moment of this drama. We have heard God's Word, made our offering with His Son, and joined in the Sacrifice. Now we prepare our souls to receive the Eucharist.[1]

The most important prayer that Jesus teaches us in Scripture is the Lord's Prayer. The priest introduces the *"Our Father"* with great humility. If it were not for Jesus' express command, we would never address God so confidently, tenderly, and directly. Through Christ, God's Son and our Brother, the first Person of the Trinity is *our* Father. As far back as the fourth century, Saint Jerome in his liturgical commentary speaks about the priest's introductory formula to the Our Father, so we know that praying this prayer in Mass is part of ancient Church tradition.

God came in the flesh to teach us how to live and how to pray. When His disciples requested of Him, *"Teach us to pray"*(cf. Lk 11: 1), He taught them the *"Our Father."* The *"Our Father"* includes all the essential elements of the perfect prayer. First, we address God as Father, just as Jesus called Him *Abba,* or *Daddy* (cf. Mk 14:36). We then pledge to respect His Holy Name, and extend His Kingdom by doing His will in our lives. This is the purpose for which we were created. But in order to do this we need His help, His love, His sustenance for our bodies and souls. So, we ask for our daily bread, bread for our bodies and the Eucharistic Bread which feeds our souls. We ask His forgiveness and promise to be forgiving. We pray for His grace to avoid falling when tempted to sin and for our ultimate deliverance from all that separates us from His love.

After the Our Father, the priest then prays for the whole community.

He prays for us to remain in peace and in true freedom. We have professed our faith, and we prepare for the Sacrament of love. This part of Mass reflects our interior yearning, as we acknowledge that we wait for the Lord's Kingdom *"with joyful hope."*

THE MOST IMPOR-
TANT PRAYER
THAT JESUS
TEACHES US IN
SCRIPTURE IS THE
LORD'S PRAYER.

A prayer that gives glory to God is called a *"doxology."* The *Glory Be* Prayer is a doxology. And after the *"Our Father"* at Mass, we pray a doxology: *"For the Kingdom, the power, and the glory are yours."* These words are not part of the *"Our Father"* in the Gospel text, but come from an early document called the *"Didache,"* or the *"Teaching of the Twelve Apostles."*

Praying to our common Father unites us as His children and family. This also reminds us that we are only united with each other in the measure that we are united in Christ and we are only united with Christ in as much as we love other people as our brothers and sisters. Our community, our communion with each other, is made lasting and complete through our communion with Christ. The *"Our Father"* is a moment for us to reflect on what should really form the basis of our community: our dedication to live as children of God,

forgiving others as we have been forgiven, and working together to do God's will and to bring humanity closer to the heavenly Kingdom.

"The peace of the Lord be with all of you."

PRAYING TO OUR COMMON FATHER UNITES US AS HIS CHILDREN AND FAMILY. THIS ALSO REMINDS US THAT WE ARE ONLY UNITED WITH EACH OTHER IN THE MEASURE THAT WE ARE UNITED IN CHRIST.

[1] *Cf. Henri Daniel-Rops, This is the Mass, (New York: Hawthorn Books, 1965) p. 138.*

CHAPTER 30

SIGN OF PEACE

T he Gospels of Matthew, Mark and Luke all narrate the institution of the Eucharist. Surprisingly, St. John does not. Since he was writing after the other Gospel writers, he decided to dedicate several chapters to everything else that Jesus did and said during the Last Supper, since the early Church already believed strongly in the Presence of Christ in the Eucharist.

At Mass, the Rite of Peace is the portion of the Communion Rite in which we ask for peace and unity for ourselves and for the whole human race. The Eucharist is the *"Sacrament of Unity,"* and as we receive Christ into our hearts we become more committed to living out Christ's message of peace and unity with others.

THE RITE OF PEACE IS THE PORTION OF THE COMMUNION RITE IN WHICH WE ASK FOR PEACE AND UNITY.

Jesus said, *"...if you bring your gift to the altar, and there recall that your brother has anything against you, leave your gift there at the altar, go first and be reconciled with your brother, and then come and offer your gift"* (cf. Mt 5:23-23). When we offer peace to our neighbor, in our hearts we must offer peace to anyone and everyone. One spiritual director was known to say, *"We love Christ - as much as we love the person we like the least."*

Christ told the apostles to wish peace upon each house they enter (cf. Lk 10:5). Jesus Himself greeted His apostles with *"Peace be with you"* when He appeared to them after His Resurrection (cf. Jn 20:19). Peace is the fruit of Jesus' Sacrifice. He died for us in order to bring us eternal peace. We are invited to receive His peace even now. The peace He gives is *not as the world gives*, but comes directly from Him and from the knowledge that He loves us and that Heaven is our destination, our hope.

When we offer peace to our neighbor, we are making a commitment to be peacemakers, who create peace around us. In the Beatitudes, Christ calls peacemakers blessed; and He assures us that, as peacemakers, we *"will be called children of God"* (cf. Mt 5:9). We hear the priest say to us: *"The peace of the Lord be with you always."* We respond, *"And with your spirit."*

In the Sermon on the Mount, Jesus told us what we need to do to be happy, or in his words, to be *"blessed."* Among His core teachings of the Beatitudes, He taught, *"Blessed are the peacemakers, for they will be called children of God"* (cf. Mt 5:9) We are God's sons and daughters by adoption in Christ. Being a Christian means being a person committed to bringing about peace. If we fulfill our commitment, we will be God's children forever.

It is only logical, then, that we offer each other peace and pray for peace for ourselves, for our neighbor, friend or foe, and for the Church and the whole world. In Mass, we do this before expressing the fullness of unity that is signified in receiving of Holy Communion.

We are all called to be holy. To be holy is to live our life like Christ's, allowing Christ to live through us. We proclaimed this in the *Gloria*. Christ's life is a life of charity. Charity is the distinctive sign of our life as Christians. St. Augustine defined peace as *"the tranquility of order."* Our lives are only truly at peace, truly tranquil, when they are ordered to God, when we live our lives for love of God. This means

we love what God loves, and we express our love of God in loving of neighbor by offering them peace.

All of this is present at the Sign of Peace. We wish our neighbor in the pew the peace that only Christ can give. We are making a commitment to live a life that only Christ can live. As the priest is the minister of the Eucharist, we all are ministers of Christ's charity and peace.

The Rite of Peace should be a renewal for us, a renewal of our commitment to live on earth as citizens of Heaven. We know we sometimes fall short of the charity of Christ, and so the priest says, *"Look not on our sins, but on the faith of your Church."* And we do not simply want earthly peace. We asked in the Lord's Prayer that God's Will would be done on earth as it is in Heaven, and now we re-echo this petition when we pray that He grant us the peace and unity of His heavenly Kingdom. In every act of love, we bring heaven to earth! And we bring others and ourselves on earth closer to Heaven!

CHAPTER 31

BREAKING OF THE BREAD—
LAMB OF GOD

Our experience at Mass parallels that of the two disciples in Scripture who were walking back to the town of Emmaus on the evening of Christ's Resurrection. While at first these men did not recognize Jesus, He began by explaining the Scriptures to them. Then they asked Him to stay with them, and finally He revealed Himself fully to them in the Breaking of the Bread. At Mass, we too have heard the Liturgy of the Word, have prayed for Christ to be with us, and now we come to know Him intimately in the Breaking of the Bread of the Eucharist.

The phrase *"Breaking of the Bread"* is the first name the early Christians used for the Mass and the Eucharist. To break bread signifies the sharing of one's life and food with family. We see each other as members of one family at the one Table of the Lord.

This Bread is Christ Himself, broken for us on the Cross. To signify this, in an act dating back to the 4th century, the priest takes and breaks the Host as Jesus did at the Last Supper. He then drops a particle into the Precious Blood to reflect the inseparability of the resurrected Lord and to symbolize the reuniting of our own glorified body and our soul in the resurrection to eternal life at Christ's Second Coming.

We recall what Scripture tells of the day St. John met Jesus, a day so etched in John's memory that over 80 years later he could recall that *"[I]t was about four in the afternoon"* (cf. Jn 1:39). John the Baptist had pointed to Jesus, Who was walking by, and said to John the future Apostle, *"Behold, the Lamb of God"* (cf. Jn 1:36). For all of Israel's history they had waited for this Lamb, for the one whose Sacrifice would take away man's sins. Christ came to save them and John believed and followed Him. Now, Christ comes to save us, to claim us, to unite us in His one Family. We are called to make an act of faith as we make our own the words of the Centurion: *"Lord, I am not worthy."* God's love is stronger than our unworthiness and He alone makes us worthy and heals us. *Truly blessed are those called to the Supper of the Lamb!*

WE HAVE HEARD THE LITURGY OF THE WORD, HAVE PRAYED FOR CHRIST TO BE WITH US, AND NOW WE COME TO KNOW HIM INTIMATELY IN THE BREAKING OF THE BREAD OF THE EUCHARIST.

The three-fold plea of the Lamb of God comes from a longer series of prayers that were said in the Eastern Churches while the consecrated Bread was being broken for distribution to the faithful. Pope St. Sergius I, a Syrian, introduced these prayers into the Mass around the year 700. In the *Agnus Dei*, the *"Lamb of God"* Prayer, we again ask for mercy, as we have done so often throughout the Mass. And we ask for the fruit of that mercy, which is peace. Christ the Lamb is offered to the Father to make reparation for our sins and those of the whole world, and to purify us making us holy.

Remembering Christ's brokenness and death is not an attempt to be morbid, but is instead recognition that He is the Source of eternal life. The priest prays, *"Lord Jesus Christ, Son of the living God, who by the will of the Father and the work of the Holy Spirit, through your death gave life to the world..."* The Body that we are preparing to receive is Christ's resurrected and glorified Body. Through communion with Him now we hope in our own resurrection with Him in Heaven.

We respond with humility to God's invitation to this banquet. Just as the centurion's faith made way for the cure of his servant in

 Scripture, our faith makes way for the healing of our own soul at Mass. The priest, staring down at the Broken Host He is about to consume, then begs for the grace of fidelity and closeness to Jesus, saying: *"Keep me always faithful to your commandments, and never let me be parted from You."*

CHAPTER 32

HOLY COMMUNION

As God prepared to deliver the people of Israel from bondage in Egypt, He ordered that they sacrifice a lamb, eat it, and sprinkle its blood on their doorposts. This would be a sign for the Angel of Death to pass over their houses, sparing them death; hence the feast of the Passover. It was not enough to simply sacrifice the lamb. They had to consume the lamb as well. This Passover meal ended with a final cup of wine, and the pronouncement, *"It is finished."* On the Cross, Jesus, expressing His thirst for souls, asked for the final Passover cup and said, *"It is finished."*

The Great Encounter has arrived. Holy Communion is a sharing in the very same meal that Jesus shared with His disciples. It is the Last Supper and the Final Passover. We all consume the same Lamb, Who is Christ Himself. He is our salvation Who saves us from death. He loved us more than His Own Life and He wanted to be with us always, so He found a way to die for us and to be with us always.

But *communion* means much more then receiving, it means *uniting*. We receive Christ in His Body and Blood, Soul and Divinity, and by this, we also *commune with Him.* We share His very life. He becomes the Food of our souls, the Life of our life. He transforms us into Himself.

Words fall far short of the depth of this mystery. The Communion songs try to express this with poetic wonderment and joy. This union is the closest and most intense communion we can have with God on earth. Heaven comes to earth; God comes to us as Food. We become one with God.

The angels surround and help the priest when he is celebrating Mass.

~ *Saint Augustine*

Through Holy Communion we draw close to Jesus and to each other. The Liturgy, after all, is the source and summit of the Christian life[1]. And after some time of silent thanksgiving, the priest, in the Prayer after Communion, asks God that the mysteries just celebrated to bear fruit in our lives. The seed of life eternal has been planted in our souls. May it bear the true fruit of love and holiness. We take a moment after returning to our pews to enjoy the Lord's company, to thank Jesus, and to tell Him that we love Him.

St. Thomas Aquinas, one of the greatest theologians in Church history, is called the *"Doctor of the Eucharist."* He wrote the Mass prayers for the Feast of Christ's Body and Blood, called *"Corpus Christi."* His own prayer after receiving Communion can help us delve deeper into the mystery of receiving Jesus in Holy Communion:

Lord, holy Father, almighty and ever-living God, I thank you. For though I am a sinner, you have fed me with the precious Body and Blood of your Son, our Lord Jesus Christ. You did this not because I deserved it, but because you are kind and merciful. I pray that this holy Communion may not add to my guilt and punishment, but may lead me to forgiveness and salvation. May it be for me the armor of faith and a shield of good will. May it purify me from evil ways and put an end to my base passions. May it bring me charity and patience, humility and obedience, and may it strengthen my power to do every kind of good. May it be a strong defense against the deceit of all my enemies, visible and invisible. May it calm perfectly all my evil impulses, bodily and spiritual. May it unite me more closely to you, the one true God; may it bring me full possession of the goal I am longing for. And I pray that you will lead me, a sinner, to the magnificent banquet where you, with your Son and the Holy Spirit are for all your saints the true light, total fulfillment, everlasting joy, gladness without end, exquisite delight, and most perfect happiness. Grant this through Christ our Lord. Amen.

[1] *Cf. Sacrosanctum Concilium, 10.*

CONCLUDING RITES

Once the Prayer after Communion is said, the Mass enters its last, brief moments, called the Concluding Rite. Indeed, we may wonder what more needs to be said or prayed. We have just offered the greatest possible act of thanksgiving to God, which is the worthy reception of the Eucharist.

WE LEAVE MASS WITH THE RESPONSIBILITY OF LIVING A LIFE IN THANKSGIVING TO GOD FOR THE GREAT LOVE HE HAS SHOWN US.

At this time some brief announcements may be given about the life of the Catholic community, often involving ways in which we can carry Christ to others through the various apostolic and charitable works of the parish.

Then the priest extends his hands, spiritually embracing his family as our father in the Faith, and gives us the final blessing, which on certain Solemnities includes a longer blessing, reminding us of the lessons of the Feast.

The deacon or priest then says, *"Go forth, the Mass is ended."* This phrase *"Ite, missa est"* is what gives the Mass, from the Latin for *"missa,"* its name. This word means a dismissal, but also a mission,

The Holy Mass would be of greater profit if people had it offered in their lifetime, rather than having it celebrated for the relief of their souls after death.

~ *Pope Benedict XV*

a sending, a commissioning. Just as Christ said to His apostles the night of His Resurrection, *"As the Father has sent me, so I send you"* (cf. Jn 20:21), we are *sent* into the world at the end of Mass.

We have encountered the Risen Lord. We leave Mass with the responsibility of living a life in thanksgiving to God for the great love He has shown us. With the Eucharist still fresh within us, with our final words *"thanks be to God,"* and with our union with our brothers and sisters in Christ expressed through song, we go forth to carry Christ in our hearts to a world that hungers for His love. We *go out (cf. Mt 26:30) to announce the Gospel of the Lord, to glorify the Lord by our life.*

P ope John Paul II's last major document was a letter to the whole Church, called an Encyclical letter, which begins, *"The Church draws her life from the Eucharist."* In his letter, he reminded us that, at Mass, we draw life from Christ in order to live the life of Christ in our world.

IF WE ACTIVELY AND CONSCIOUSLY PARTICIPATE IN MASS WELL, GRACE WILL TRANSFORM OUR LIVES, AND THROUGH US CHRIST WILL TRANSFORM THE WORLD.

After Jesus' Resurrection, the apostles were still fearful, even though their faith brought them back to the Upper Room where they had been with Jesus at the Last Supper. But, when the Holy Spirit descended upon them and strengthened them, they rose in courage and enthusiasm, taking to the streets. St. Peter, the same Peter who denied Jesus three times after the Last Supper, goes forth at Pentecost boldly proclaiming the Resur-rection, teaching: *"God raised this Jesus; of this we are all witnesses"* (cf. Acts 2:32).

Each and every Mass, as we have seen, is an experience of Christmas, of Christ coming into the world. It is a reliving of Good Friday, Christ's dying on the Cross for us. It is an experience of the Resurrection, as Christ's Risen Body and Blood becomes our

Food. But, Mass must also be for us a new Pentecost, when we *"are clothed with power from on high"* (cf. Lk 24:49) and are blessed with the fire of love, which we are to carry to our homes, schools, places of business, even to the ends of the earth.

Three things are necessary for the salvation of man: to know what he ought to believe; to know what he ought to desire; and to know what he ought to do.

~ Saint Thomas Aquinas

Like the wise men, our hearts are on fire for the Truth. We have searched and discovered Truth and Love. Every Mass is a limitless source of holiness and grace. If we actively and consciously participate in Mass well, and build our lives around the lessons learned in what has been called the *"school of the Eucharist,"* grace will transform our lives, and through us Christ will transform the world.

So, let us be like St. Martha who courageously and with humble confidence engaged our Lord Jesus concerning the death of her brother Lazarus, pleading:

Lord if you had been here my brother would not have died. And even now I know that whatever you ask from God, God will give you.

And hear Him say to her:

Your brother will rise again.

Listening as she responds:

I know that he will rise again in the resurrection on the last day.

Seeing how Jesus confirms Who He is and His mission:

I am the resurrection and the life; he who believes in me, even though he dies, shall live, and whoever lives and believes in me shall never die.

And then hearing Him ask Martha, as He also now asks us:

Do you believe this?

While we join Martha in saying with all our hearts:

Yes, Lord; I believe that you are the Christ, the Son of God, who has come into the world.

*"See what love the Father has
bestowed on us that we may be called
the children of God. Yet so we are."*

(cf. 1 Jn 3:1)